Did God Create Sports Also?

Did God Create Sports Also?

Thinking Christianly About Sports

By Robert G. Spinney

Did God Create Sports Also? Thinking
Christianly About Sports
ISBN 0-9776680-3-7

1st Edition
Copyright © 2006 by Robert G. Spinney
All rights reserved.

Tulip Books
P.O. Box 481
Hartsville, TN 37074 USA
www.tulipbooks.com

All Scripture quotations are from the
New American Standard Bible
© The Lockman Foundation 1960, 1962, 1963, 1968,
1971, 1972, 1973, 1975, 1977. Used by permission.

The year is 1500. You enter any large Western European city and one building captures your attention: the cathedral. This enormous and beautiful structure is the pride of the city. The local residents sacrificially contribute large sums of money (in the form of offerings and special gifts) to fund its construction. Cities are often known by their famous cathedrals: Notre Dame in Paris, Saint Peter's in Rome, Saint Paul's in London, Saint Vitus in Prague. The cathedrals serve as tangible expressions of what is important to almost every medieval European: religion. As the most distinctive and popular building in the city, the cathedral memorializes in concrete and stone the kinds of things that are able to inflame the passions of medieval Europeans.

The year is 2000. You enter any large American city and one building captures your attention: the sports stadium. This enormous and beautiful structure is the pride of the city. The local residents sacrificially contribute large sums of money (in the form of bonds and special tax exemptions) to fund its construction. Cities are often known by their famous stadiums: the Superdome in New Orleans, Fenway Park in Boston, Lambeau Field in Green Bay, Yankee Stadium in New York City. The stadiums serve as tangible expressions of what is important to almost every American: sports. As the most distinctive and popular building in the city, the sports stadium memorializes in concrete and stone the kinds of things that are able to inflame the passions of modern-day Americans.

Of course, sports are not new. Native American Indians played a form of lacrosse and ancient Greeks held Olympic games. What is new is the place of importance that sports occupy in America today.

Every morning, millions of Americans begin their day by turning first to the sports section of their morning newspapers. People identify themselves by referencing sports, both in speech ("Hi, I'm Frank. I'm a computer programmer and a Los Angeles Laker fan.") and by wearing clothing that contains sports logos. (In Georgia, wearing a University of Florida hat is a bold public declaration regarding one's identity.) Sports stars are used to sell merchandise, endorse politicians, encourage morality, promote charitable giving, and keep children away from drugs. Athletic metaphors are staples in our language: "Your business presentation was a slam dunk." "Conservative judges support a three-strikes-you're-out rule for repeat offenders." "I don't know what to do, so I think we should punt." Businessmen wearing ties give one another high fives and chest bumps.

Children's reading and math skills are declining, but the time they spend in organized youth sports is increasing. A recent survey revealed that American high schoolers spend an average of thirteen hours per week participating in athletics and less than five hours per week on homework. Few things can turn a family's schedule upside down more than involvement in Little League sports. A mother's life may be so dominated by ferrying children to practices and games that her year seems to consist of only three seasons: soccer season, football season, and baseball season. Youth sports coaches are even becoming trusted role models in our culture. According to a recent survey of the American public, 45 percent said that they trusted Catholic priests, 66 percent said that they trusted Protestant ministers, and 68 percent reported that they trusted adults who serve as Little League sports coaches.

One way to measure the value we place upon sports is to look at the salaries of professional athletes. The average professional baseball player today earns $2.5 million per year; by comparison, the average salary for a policeman is $50,000 per year. When we pay a man who hits a baseball fifty times more than a man who risks his life dealing with criminals, we demonstrate what is important to us as a culture. Or consider television commercials. The most expensive advertising time on American television is during professional football's Super Bowl. In 2005, a thirty-second-long slot sold for about $2 million; all fifty-nine commercial opportunities were sold. (That compares to $400,000 for a comparable slot during normal prime-time programming.)

How do politicians spend money? In 1990, the elected leaders of Oakland, California, ignored declining schools, street violence, and unhealthy ghettoes when they pledged $100 million to lure their departed professional football team back to the city. The Raiders were apparently more important than these other urban needs: when the attempt to reclaim the team failed, the $100 million disappeared and was unavailable for other civic purposes. Why do politicians allocate money like this? Because we Americans have a value system in place, a value system that reveals an obsession with sports. "In a capitalist culture, money is how you keep score," observes theologian Cornelius Plantinga. "By this barometer, we value amusement more than good law, medicine, government, ministry, education, architecture, or scientific research." (*Not the Way It's Supposed to Be: A Breviary of Sin*, p. 190.)

What does it mean to think Christianly about sports? How should Christians respond to our national obsession with sports?

Christians seem to have stopped asking these questions a long time ago. To even suggest that God's people should examine their relationship to sports is to raise eyebrows. But surely an issue as large as recreation deserves a biblical response. The Bible instructs Christians not to be conformed to this world's way of thinking (Romans 12:1-2). That means we must not be squeezed into the world's mold. We should not accept blindly our culture's understanding of anything, including hobbies, politics, vulgar speech, or care for the elderly. Nor should we simply assume that our culture uses sports as God intended them to be used. We must think Christianly about the subjects of entertainment and physical recreation. Like work, marriage, child-rearing, and education, this area of life must be taken captive to the obedience of Christ and submitted to His lordship (2 Corinthians 10:5).

Surely Abraham Kuyper's famous dictum applies to sports: "There is not a square inch in the whole domain of our human existence over which Christ, who is sovereign over all, does not cry: 'Mine!'"

So what are some biblical guidelines that shed light on this issue of Christians and sports?

1 Sports are a part of God's good creation. They can both glorify God and profit our souls.

In the same sense that God invented music and art, He also invented sports. God created humans with the capacity and inclination to engage in athletic endeavors. Just as music is man's developing of abilities and desires that

God created in humans, so sports are man's cultivating of abilities and desires that God planted in humans. Like music and art, sports are God's good gifts to mankind. God could have created humans with neither inclination nor ability to engage in physical recreation, but He didn't. Instead, He planted the seeds of creative and expressive activities inside us, including recreational activities. Because God is a God of purpose, it is reasonable to infer that He deliberately created mankind with these innate capacities so that we might develop them.

When we pursue athletics in a godly manner, it is part of our subduing of (or exercising dominion over) God's creation: it is subduing that part of God's creation that is resident inside man himself.

Music and art can be done properly. So can sports. When sports are brought under the lordship of Christ and done to the glory of God, they contribute to the richness of life on earth. They can be a source of legitimate pleasure. They can promote good health. They can provide refreshing distractions from daily routines, distractions that Puritan poet John Milton called "delightful intermissions" of "joy and harmless pastime." They can create meaningful family times. They can encourage the development of self-discipline, cooperation, perseverance, and other biblical virtues. Puritan pastor William Perkins argued that moderate recreation made a man a better laborer. According to Eric Liddell (of *Chariots of Fire* fame), sports can sometimes encourage a man to worship: Liddell said that when he ran, he could feel God's pleasure.

Sports are best regarded as a means to a greater end. As our spiritual forefathers put it so well, the chief end of man is to glorify God and enjoy Him forever. Recreation (like every other good gift that God gives) is a means to that end. It is a way to better outfit man for his chief end of bringing glory to God. Note the literal sense of this word recreation: it denotes a re-creation. It speaks of a refreshing and a rejuvenation that enables a person to regain original strength, vigor, and acuity. The man who uses sports as God intends is re-created and refreshed. He is better able to glorify God, serve God, and extend God's kingdom. When our sports are a means to the end of glorifying God, it is likely that our sports are both legitimate and spiritually beneficial.

In the past, wise Christians put these two truths together. They said that if God created man with the capacity and inclination to engage in recreation, and if we can identify spiritual benefits that result from participation in sports, then it is actually *necessary* for Christians to engage in recreation. "Let us know," wrote John Downame, a Puritan pastor from the 1600s, "that honest recreation is a thing not only lawful, but also profitable and necessary." The famous Richard Baxter, another Puritan pastor, agreed. "No doubt but some sport and recreation is lawful, yea needful," advised Baxter, "and therefore a duty to some men." What kinds of sports did the Puritans enjoy? A short list would include archery, shooting, running, wrestling, leaping, fencing, bowling, swimming, ice skating, football, bat-and-ball games, hunting, and fishing.

The old Puritans had it right: sports are part of the fullness and blessedness of God's creation.

The Apostle Paul once gave Christians counsel regarding food that had been sacrificed previously to idols. He concluded his words by writing, "Whether, then, you eat or drink or whatever you do, do all to the glory of God" (1 Corinthians 10:31). In the final analysis, said Paul, glorifying God is your primary purpose for being on earth; make sure that whatever you do is part of fulfilling that mission. Nothing should prevent or obscure others from seeing God's glory reflected in you. The ultimate test regarding eating, drinking, or engaging in a sport is whether it results in God being further glorified.

Can we engage in sports and recreation in such a way that God is glorified? Yes.

2 We can engage in recreation in such a way that it doesn't glorify God and doesn't bless us.

The sad reality of our sinful condition is that we humans can take God's good gifts and corrupt them. Our sin can poison our musical and artistic efforts so that they are neither pleasing to God nor helpful to men. The same is true for our athletic efforts. God-given abilities and desires that were intended to profit us can become ways that we express our sin. "As a result of sin," observes Arthur Holmes, a longtime professor of philosophy at Wheaton College, "leisure has become laziness and play self-indulgence; players are exploited, and the playful life is perverted." (*Contours of a World View*, p. 231)

Sports are often corrupted by failing to regard them as a means to the end of glorifying God. When our sports are not linked to the greater good of glorifying God, they become ends (or goals) in themselves. Instead of enjoying God, pursuing things that God values, or refreshing oneself for future service to God, the goal becomes the praise of men, escape from legitimate responsibilities, the adrenaline rush of beating someone, an attractive body, or unbridled pleasure. As long as our recreations are linked to God, they possess built-in criteria that help us put boundaries around our sports: our sports are out-of-bounds when they no longer assist us in glorifying God. But when recreation and God are un-linked, the built-in criteria disappear; it becomes less clear when our sports are out-of-bounds. Indeed, if the goal of my sports participation is simply maximizing my pleasure, then who is to say that I am spending too much money or too much time on my sports? The goal (maximizing pleasure) implies criteria (as much money and time as it takes to produce pleasure).

This is not a dynamic unique to sports; indeed, it appears in many legitimate human activities. God gives us material gifts so that we might better serve Him, but we become consumed with the gift and forget the Giver. We crave more and bigger gifts, losing sight of God Himself. God gives us physical abilities so that we might better serve Him, but we become obsessed with our strengths and skills. Instead of glorifying God and employing our abilities in His service, we become proud of our prowess and use it to serve ourselves. So too in recreation: when we no longer engage in sports in order to better serve God, our recreation often functions as a mini-god.

This becomes a kind of spiritual cancer: God gives us recreation in order to glorify Him more fully, we neglect the end of glorifying God, we use recreation for other purposes, and our recreation swells up like a cancerous tumor . . . a grotesque tumor that crowds God out of our lives. It displaces and sometimes replaces God.

3 We misuse sports when they (not God) address our deepest needs and become our purpose in life.

Idolatry is much more than worshipping little statues. Idolatry is attempting to meet deep and fundamental needs through a substitute god (that is, any thing other than God). By deep and fundamental needs, I mean things like our need for a sense of purpose in our lives, our need to be committed to something worthwhile, our need to find fulfillment, our need to feel like we are worth something, and our need to feel good about ourselves. This is what idols do: they attempt to meet these fundamental human needs. They promise us things that only God can give us. They service misplaced longings.

Of course, simply enjoying something or allocating time to something doesn't necessarily make that thing an idol. Enthusiastic engagement in an activity doesn't always constitute idolatry. Idols are more powerful than this: they dominate our lives and define us. When something is my idol, I can't imagine living without it. I cherish it dearly. I will make sacrifices for it and protect it fiercely. I will think longingly about it during my free time. And in everyday situations, I will prioritize my idol over doing the things that God requires. Some potential idols might include jobs, families, hobbies, prestige, physical appearance, and bank accounts. A growing number of Christians today are asking, "Are sports the idols of choice among twenty-first century Americans?"

How do I know if sports have become my idol?

If I consistently organize my life around my recreation, then my recreation may well be idolatrous. Have you noticed that no matter how busy we are, we usually end up making time for those things that are really important to us? The essential things usually win when it comes to schedule conflicts. It is likely that sports functions as my idol if the priorities in my schedule persistently revolve around recreation.

Sports is my idol if I can't imagine living without it. Some people have weekly routines that include a sizeable dose of recreation. Perhaps without knowing it, participating in or watching sports is a way that they manage their mood. It keeps them more or less content. It allows them to escape from responsibility and pressure. The thought of spending a week with no television and hence no sports strikes them as almost scary. Normal life requires that they have their fix of sports. Sound farfetched? A sports radio station recently asked its listeners, "If somebody offered you $2 million, could you give up all sports for two years?" One listener phoned in and said no. "It's where I turn when I pick up the paper in the morning. It's where I go when I'm on the internet. It's what I watch on television. It's what I listen to on the radio in the car. Everywhere I go, it surrounds everything I do." (Sounds like this person has an omnipresent idol.)

Sports is my idol if I cherish it more than anything else. Only the rare individual would ever say, "I love recreation more than I love God." But our loves are revealed by our actions. Our behavior indicates what we love (and what we don't love!). For example, we sacrifice for the things that we love: how do your sacrifices for sports compare to your sacrifices for God's kingdom? We defend fiercely the things that we love: do you defend church issues as zealously as you defend sports issues? We want to learn more about the things that we love: do you know more about soccer than you do about the doctrine of justification by faith alone?

Sports is my idol if I consistently get passionate over sports but regard serving God as painful or boring. We are not talking merely about fun here. Christianity is not entertainment, and recreation involves amusement in a way that serving God does not. We are talking about passion— about committed, intense, engaged, and sustained desire. After all, passion is another indicator of what we love and what interests us. We get passionate over things that are important to us. It is difficult to manufacture passion; it simply appears when we are pursuing our heart's deepest desires. Which is greater: your enthusiasm for the things of God or your enthusiasm for sports? Are you passionate about your recreation but bored when it comes to serving the Lord Jesus Christ?

The issue at stake here is much deeper than just sports. Why would I regard some thing in my life as indispensable, love it intensely, consistently get passionate over it, feel fulfilled when I am engaged in it, and organize my schedule around it? I only make this kind of whole-person commitment to something when I think that it really meets my deepest needs. Any thing that occupies this kind of place in my life (whether it is a sport, a job, a vice, a hobby, or a little statue) is a substitute god. It is an idol.

4 *Sports do not glorify God when they distract us from biblical behaviors and require too much time.*

Idols compete with the true God. They are rival gods. What happens when sporting events or recreation competes with God in your life?

If we miss church services, Bible studies, prayer meetings, or other spiritual activities because of sports, our sports are far too important. God never created recreation so that it might compete with (and supplant) the church or the teaching of the Bible!

Pastors are hearing something today that they didn't hear forty years ago: "We won't be at church meetings this coming Sunday. Billy has a soccer game." When kicking a soccer ball is regarded as more important than worshipping God and hearing God's Word taught, sports are too big. "But Billy's absence will let his teammates down." You and Billy have a commitment to the Lord Jesus Christ and His church that is far more critical than any commitment to Little League teammates; your absence from the Body of Christ will let the church down. "But Billy's soccer is his ticket to a college scholarship." What will it profit Billy if he gains the whole college scholarship but loses his own soul? Parents, demonstrate to your children what it means to seek first the kingdom of God and His righteousness (Matthew 6:33). Your children should see that your priorities rest with God's kingdom.

Churches are facing something today that they didn't face forty years ago: church members simply don't attend church meetings because a big game is on television or they have tickets to a local sporting event. Sadly, it is trendy today to discredit church attendance as an old-fashioned idea that (if presented as something essential to Christian health) is legalistic. But God has created the local church as a kind of spiritual greenhouse where His people flourish (Ephesians 4:1-16). God has also given Spirit-endowed men to serve as pastor-teachers of these churches. God Himself says that the local church is extremely important; His Word commands us to not forsake our assembling together (Hebrews 10:25). If we are neglecting what God says is important, the bottom line is quite simple: which is more important, the game or God?

Recreation costs a lot of money. I gasp when I see the price of tickets for sporting events. Membership in health clubs is expensive. Not only are there fees to register your children in youth sports leagues, but there are the added costs of youth sports equipment, transportation, and restaurant meals due to chaotic schedules. True sports fans must have team shirts, hats, jackets, mugs, key chains, seat cushions, and license plates. For a hefty fee, you can purchase a special television package that will bring up to 200 professional football games into your home over the seventeen-week-long football season. Since athletic recreation is one of God's good gifts to man, it is entitled to some portion of the money that God entrusts to us. Good financial stewardship may well result in modest expenditures on sports. But surely it is possible to squander God's money foolishly on sports. Do you cheerfully allocate money to recreation and grudgingly allocate money to God's work? When the kingdom of God and the kingdom of sports compete for your money, who wins?

How much time do you devote to sports and recreation? As God's good gifts, they are surely entitled to some of your time. But do they dominate your schedule? Do they disrupt your family, making it difficult to eat meals together? Do they consume so much time that you are left with insufficient time to do other needful things? Take this quick test. Estimate how much time you spend per week engaging in recreational activities, watching sports on television or from bleachers, and ferrying children back and forth from sporting events. Two hours? Four hours? More? Now estimate how much time you spend per week reading the Bible, praying, and meditating on God's Word. What happens when the kingdom of God and the kingdom of sports compete for your time? Which one wins?

Enjoy recreation as God's good gift if it is a rejuvenating break from the main business of life. If sports better equips you to extend God's kingdom, fulfill your family obligations, and labor honorably for your employer, then by all means make use of what Milton called God's "delightful intermissions." But repent of a modern form of Baal worship—ball worship—if recreation causes you to evade your moral responsibility to worship God, nurture your family, help others, care for your soul, use your time wisely, or otherwise glorify God and enjoy Him forever. "The sports god is an enticing deity," writes Mark Galli. "He offers splendid moments of transcendence while never demanding that we take up our cross, forgive our enemies, or serve the poor. No wonder that we sometimes spend too much time with this benign god." ("The Prodigal Sports Fan," *Christianity Today*, 8 April 2005)

This is not an anti-sports argument; rather, it is a pro-God argument. In your life, you will encounter many potential rival gods. They will compete with the true God for your commitment, time, money, and devotion. Many of them, like work, family, friends, education, and recreation, are legitimate God-sanctioned things . . . provided that they don't crowd God out of your life and become your true love. Surely the Holy One of Israel must win these showdowns with potential idols.

5 *Our sports do not glorify God when they nurture in us an excessive and unhealthy competitiveness.*

Athletic competition can be salutary. It can be a means whereby we develop self-discipline, teamwork skills, a healthy work ethic, and problem-solving abilities. In a free enterprise economy, earning one's living often involves at least a measure of righteous competition; athletics can help nurture such a life skill. Good-natured competition among friends can be invigorating and refreshing. Some competition is really only a harmless device whereby friends enjoy one another's company and perhaps encourage one another to pursue excellence.

But increasingly, sports in America nurture a competitiveness that is unhealthy. Athletes trash talk their opponents. They don't just try to win; they try to humiliate their opponents and crush them. They taunt. They get angry at their teammates for playing poorly. They argue, lose their tempers, and throw things when referees make unfavorable decisions. (Our culture only tolerates temper tantrums on sports playing fields and in toddlers' playpens.) Youth sports coaches yell at players and berate them for poor performances. Parents are sometimes worse than their children when it comes to abusive speech at sporting events. (Will the Holy Spirit really lead you to boo umpires and heckle opposing players?) Surely this is out-of-control competitiveness. It nurtures in us sins like anger, hatred, pride, blame-shifting, and a lack of compassion. We are not displaying peace, kindness, gentleness, and self-control when we compete like this.

One famous athlete triumphed over his opponent and began shouting, "I am the greatest! I am the greatest!" He glared sinisterly at his defeated opponent and beat his chest proudly. "I am the greatest in the world!" he bellowed. This was more than just an emotional victory celebration: this was boastful self-exaltation and a proud display of egoism. Unfortunately, this kind of ego exaggeration is now commonplace even among eight-year-old t-ball players. When they hit a home run or make a good catch, they mimic the athletes they see on television: they strut, congratulate themselves, beat their chests, taunt their opponents, and expect public adoration. At some point, egotistical victory celebrations make a mockery of the biblical virtue of humility. Self-exalting Christians are disobedient Christians. Success in competition does not justify sinful pride. Taunting is not a fruit of the Spirit.

A famous football coach once said, "Winning isn't everything. It's the only thing." Indeed, winning has become so important that athletes cheat and deceive. They take illegal performance-enhancing drugs. They tell the umpire the pitch hit them when it didn't. One ice skater hired a thug to injure the knee of her opponent. One all-star hockey player remained a perennial fan favorite despite his history of cheap shots, which included deliberately hitting an opposing player in the mouth with his hockey stick and driving his stick bayonet-style into an opponent's groin. Sadly, even athletes who profess to be Christians sometimes compete like this.

Competition marked by this kind of behavior does not glorify God. As an athlete, I must restrain my competitiveness so that I don't sin; if I can't do that, I must flee this temptation like any other temptation that leads me into sinful behaviors. As a sports fan, I can't derive entertainment from athletes' unbiblical conduct. When we enjoy the bloody fistfight that breaks out during a hockey game, are we enjoying God-glorifying recreation or are we rejoicing in unrighteousness?

The Lord Jesus Christ began the Sermon on the Mount with the words, "Blessed are the poor in spirit, for theirs is the kingdom of heaven." He followed with, "Blessed are the gentle [or meek], for they shall inherit the earth." (Matthew 5:3,5) It is possible for Christians to engage in athletic competition while still obeying Christ's command to be poor in spirit and gentle. However, athletic competition does not provide God's people with an exemption from these commands. Arrogance and boastfulness are still sins (Romans 1:30). God's condemnation of violence still stands (Genesis 6:11, Psalm 11:5, Proverbs 3:31). Of special concern is competition that cultivates within the athlete (or fan) less poverty of spirit, less gentleness, and less meekness. When this happens, athletic competition actually trains us in unrighteousness. God is not glorified in this; we are not benefitted by this.

6 *For many, sports expose how we behave when we love something and are deeply committed to it.*

When I was eleven years old, my father took me to a Chicago Bears football game.

The game was on my mind long before we got there. The night before, I could scarcely sleep due to my excitement. But I managed to fall asleep, and we awoke early the next morning. No one had to drag me out of my bed! It was a cold and windy day in Chicago, and my father and I prepared for the game. We ate a big breakfast. We packed food. We dressed warmly and took extra blankets. We left our house early in the morning because it was a long drive to old Soldier Field, and we knew there would be additional game-day traffic. Parking was a nightmare, so we trekked many blocks to the stadium along with the other Bears faithful. The wind was howling! We bent over as we walked, straining against the wind and under the load of all our game supplies. At last, we arrived at the stadium and found our seats. Although it had taken us over two hours to drive into the city, find a parking place, and hike to our seats, we were there long before kick-off time. There was no way we were going to be late for the game: it was too important!

The game was great. We screamed and cheered for over three hours. No boredom here: our attention was riveted on the field. It was freezing outside on the cold metal bleacher seats, and the wind whipped through the outdoor stadium. But we didn't mind. We enjoyed fellowship with the strangers seated around us, as we were bound together by our common love of football. We were actually a little sad when the final horn sounded and the game came to an end. (We would have loved to have stayed for overtime and another twenty minutes of football.) We slowly filed out of the stadium and then shuffled along the sidewalks with thousands of other fans to our car. Thanks to the traffic jam around the football stadium, we inched our way toward home. My dad and I talked football the whole way home, reliving the game's highlights. We finally arrived at our house well after dark.

The game had taken the entire day. We had adjusted our schedules to make time for it. The tickets and downtown parking were expensive. We were cold and tired.

Do you know why my father and I did this? Because we loved it! We were passionate about football. And today (some thirty-five years later) I look back on that event and see some important things about myself.

When I really love something, I don't mind making sacrifices for it. In fact, what other people might call sacrifices (e.g., the expensive tickets, the cold weather, the long drive) were things that I deemed minor inconveniences.

When something is truly important to me, I'm not bored by it. During our long pre-game preparation, expectation extinguished boredom. During our long post-game ride home, memories overwhelmed boredom. Interest generates desire and passion.

When I am passionate about something, I don't need to be forced to do it. No one had to coerce me to go to that football game! I eagerly invested much time and effort in my sports; I was not a reluctant sports fan. Enthusiasm is an effective motivator.

When I really enjoy something, time is not a factor. I never complained that the football game was too long. Time flies when you're doing what you love.

When I find other people who share my passion, we enjoy a special bond of friendship. My father and I made friends with complete strangers at that Chicago Bears game. Common commitment creates warm fellowship.

When something brings me great joy and satisfaction, I become evangelistic. Do you know what I did the day after I saw the Bears game? I told all my friends. I looked for someone who was willing to listen; I was bursting at the seams with a need to share my experience. Excitement translates into telling others.

I attended that Chicago Bears game a long time ago. However, it presents a challenge to me today: is that how I love the Lord Jesus Christ? That football game demonstrates how I behave when I am passionate about something; am I truly passionate about the kingdom of God? That game demonstrates how I act when something is important to me; is following the Lord Jesus Christ truly important to me?

Professor Richard O. Davies is a historian who has studied American sports extensively. He concludes his recent book *America's Obsession: Sports and Society Since 1945* with these thought-provoking words: "Sports in modern America has taken on a significance greater than the wins and losses reported in the daily newspapers, becoming a powerful metaphor for life in the United

States. Recalling his teenage years during the late 1940s, [Pulitzer Prize winning journalist] David Halberstam writes, 'The world of baseball seemed infinitely more real and appealing than the world around me.... Encouraged by [radio announcer] Mel Allen and countless sportswriters, I believed that I knew the Yankees not only as players but as people— they were part of my extended family.'" Then Davies offers this penetrating insight: "Halberstam captures one of the essential qualities of sports. They provide Americans with a safe and comfortable haven in an often confusing, unstable, and disturbing world....Caught up in this era of turbulent change and vast uncertainty, many Americans have found a refuge in sports. The void often left unfilled by politics, work, family, or religion has been at least partially filled by an increased involvement in the world of sports" (pp. 254-255).

Although Davies is discussing sports here, he is also discussing concepts relevant to theology. For good reason, Christians often speak of havens, refuges, and unfilled voids. Because of our own sin and the sin that permeates the world around us, we live in a world that Davies aptly characterizes as confusing, unstable, and disturbing. This is a part of our common condition as sinful men. We long for fulfillment and seek satisfaction. We discover that a kind of void exists inside us, and we desperately attempt to fill that void with all kinds of things (including sports). We seek refuge in worldly remedies so often that we do it subconsciously. We hope our remedies will give us the contentment and peace that we crave. But they leave us dissatisfied, still searching for a safe and comfortable haven.

That's because only the Lord Jesus Christ creates true fulfillment within a man's soul. Other refuges will fail us;

only the spiritual haven that we find in Christ is truly satisfying. The crucified and risen Messiah knows how to meet our deepest needs. The Son of God can work supernaturally inside us to fill the God-shaped void in our souls. He alone deserves to be the priority in our life; He alone may command the first place in our schedules. Sports are useful, but when they become idols, they do what all idols do: they make false promises, deceive us, steal our time, and leave us empty. Not so with the Good Shepherd: He came that we might have life and might have it abundantly (John 10:10).

OTHER TITLES FROM TULIP BOOKS

HOW TO SURVIVE YOUR PASTOR'S SERMONS: Six Ways to Make Pulpit Messages More Profitable to Your Soul

A faithful church attender will hear about fifty pastoral sermons every year. That translates into 500 sermons every decade. If you are a Christian for forty years, you will likely hear about 2,000 sermons from a pulpit. When we add to this count all the conference messages, sermons on audio tape, and other pulpit messages to which you will listen, the number climbs even higher. Do you benefit from these times when you hear God's Word proclaimed? Do you wish to benefit more?

This booklet addresses these questions. It is designed for the Christian who wants to receive maximum spiritual benefit from the pulpit sermons and Bible lessons he hears. An earnest pastor can "preach well" and make it more likely that the Holy Spirit will illuminate the Bible during his sermon; likewise, an earnest listener can "hear well" and make it more likely that he will be transformed by his exposure to the Word of God. This booklet will help you to have ears that hear.

WHAT IS THE MEANING OF BAPTISM? A Guide For Christians Preparing For Baptism

What should a new Christian know before he gets baptized? Is baptism simply a ceremony where we obey the Bible's command, or is there a need to understand the meaning of baptism? What rich spiritual truths does God communicate in baptism that (if understood) result in the believer realizing spiritual benefits from this ordinance?

This booklet addresses these questions. It is a short and easy-to-understand explanation of believer's baptism. The booklet is written for the new Christian who wants to be baptized. It emphasizes that baptism is a picture of both the believer's union with the risen Christ and the believer's saving response to the gospel. Past Christians wisely characterized baptism as a visible gospel message because it embodies the central truths of salvation in the Lord Jesus Christ. Understand baptism and you understand the heart of the gospel.

Pastors will find this a useful tool as they prepare new believers for baptism.

PEEKING INTO THE DEVIL'S PLAYBOOK: Satan's Strategies for Tempting Christians to Sin

Temptation is a nearly forgotten topic among Christians today. This is unfortunate, as Satan's primary activity in this present world is tempting believers to sin. Thus for the healthy saint, resisting temptation must be a daily spiritual discipline.

This booklet is based upon (and introduces the reader to) Thomas Brooks's classic Puritan book *Precious Remedies Against Satan's Devices*. The booklet follows the structure of the opening section of Brooks's book: it identifies and explains twelve common tactics that Satan uses to tempt Christians to sin. The emphasis is upon understanding both temptation and God's "precious remedies" that enable the saint to escape Satan's snares.

Spiritual warfare is an often misunderstood topic. This booklet examines the day-to-day aspect of spiritual warfare. On the one hand, Satan wars against the Christian by tempting him to sin; on the other hand, the saint wars against Satan by fighting temptation and pursuing holiness.

MONKEYING AROUND WITH DANGEROUS IDEAS:
Four Reasons Outside the Field of Science Why Christians
Should Reject Evolutionary Thinking

Christians should reject the theory of evolution because it is both untrue and bad science. But there are other reasons — reasons from outside the field of science — why believers should affirm the biblical account of creation. This booklet briefly examines how Darwinism erodes faith in the trustworthiness of the Bible, undermines Scripture's explanation of how the Lord Jesus Christ saves lost men, promotes a naturalistic worldview that is hostile to the Christian worldview, and assaults the essential dignity of humans (which leads to immoral conduct).

Even the men who champion evolution admit that it is much more than a scientific theory. They frankly concede that it fuels an entire worldview, one that affects thinking about politics, religion, morality, and human worth. That's why followers of the Lord Jesus Christ must be alert to the numerous evolution-driven presuppositions, values, and judgments that are widespread in the West today.

6 — eat ginger